The

Art of Giving

ZERO FUCKS

THE GREATEST APPROACH TO STAYING HAPPY

MATT MILLER

Table of Contents

Introduction

Not giving a fuck is not about being indifferent. It suggests you are okay with being different. Don't say fuck it to everything in life, just to the unimportant things. To not give a fuck about adversity, you must first care about something more fundamental than difficulties. Whether you realize it or not, you are continually determining what to give a fuck about. The goal is to gradually prune the things you care about so that you only give a fuck on the most critical of occasions.

Not giving a fuck is not a justification for you to be a reckless jerk; it is also not about entirely rejecting what is happening across the world.

Nihilism is the view that everything is useless. It is a belief in nothing, that ultimate destruction is good. And understanding how to not give a fuck is not about that.

The genuine meaning of not giving fucks is identifying where you should give a fuck. Let's face it, you don't have an unlimited quantity of fucks. A fuck is a rare resource that you need to utilize properly. The reality is that everyone gives a fuck about something. Money. Power. Sex. Status. Whatever. It is impossible not to give a fuck about anything.

The problem is that too many of us give too many fucks about the things that are not vital and that don't matter. The things we can't control and can't modify such as the perspectives of others, what other people think of us, and whether or not someone else likes us.

What we should be doing is prioritizing our fucks for the things that matter. Before we go further, let's explain what a "fuck" is:

The definition of a "fuck"
Giving a fuck says you care. When I say I don't give a fuck about football, I mean I don't care about football. Now let's take the concept a step further: Let's define your fucks as your time, energy, and money.

I love this definition.

So what are the things that we should and shouldn't give a fuck about?

The sort of stuff you should give a fuck about;
Your profession, business, time, money, health, happiness, friends, family, and so on.

The sort of stuff you shouldn't give a fuck about;
What other people think of you
Whether or not other people like you
The ideas of random persons on social media
The things you can't control and can't influence

The expectations of others – unless it is your employer or your customers

The perspectives of others – especially those who don't know what the heck they are talking about

Celebrity gossip

The newest trends

Approval seeking

Putting Yourself First

Learning how to stop caring is not as uncomplicated as you may imagine. It is human nature, although training yourself on how to not care may be precisely what you need. It might seem weird to learn how to stop caring. We spend our whole lives doing the opposite. Training oneself on how to not care is dreadful. But, we all know that person who looks to be able to let things roll off of their backs so easily. You know, the one who just doesn't care. They are just unabashed themselves.

If you are the opposite and struggle to let things go, you may have to retrain your brain. And it won't be easy. Society, media, and even our family have educated us to care about what others think. We want to come off in a particular manner. Caring is what suggests that you are devoted, putting effort in, and wish to impress others.

This could be hard to endure if you are already a sensitive person. It may rapidly become a difficult way to live. Bound by worrying about what others think and whether or not they are judging you. It is simple to become neurotic and socially awkward. To stop living with such anxiety and learn how not to care, you need to shift your mindset, which is much easier said than done.

Caring Too Much

This may seem silly, but stay with me. Caring is not a weakness. Let me just start with that. Caring suggests you have a nice heart. But, you carry the defects of the world around with you. This weighs you down. It means you encourage others and let yourself fall. You've learned to care for others. That is a good thing. You don't want to get rid of it. The point is, if you are here, it means you probably care too much. Why is that? Well, caring too much arises when you lack limitations.

For instance, you care for your partner. But, when you break up, you still care for them. It is not merely that you care that they are well, but you care if they are suffering and want to remedy their sorrow even when you don't actually want to be with them. You let your compassion for others go above and beyond your concern for yourself. That is where the trouble exists.

When you allow your concern for others to transgress limitations, you are disrespecting yourself. You are prioritizing the happiness and calm of others above your peace of mind, mental health, and enjoyment. You are caring for inconsiderate people, and it is eating away at you.

The Right Amount of Care

If you want to know how to stop caring, it actually is about making some basic alterations in your belief system. Knowing how to not care is about liberating oneself from the weight of continuously trying to please others and putting limitless amounts of effort in. It is your life and you should do what you choose.

With that being mentioned, you don't need to become an apathetic and cruel person who goes through life simply worrying about oneself. What you want is to find a balance between caring and not caring too much. And, this is how...

1. Stop caring about other people's judgments

Everyone judges. It is human nature.

It is really in our genetic constitution. Judging people originates from our inherent drive to put things into categories. It is a survival technique that we employ to aid us assess if something is a hazard.

Judging alone is not the problem.

Judging without needed cause, however, is. This is when we are sucked down. When someone criticizes you based on your dress or style, you feel like fuck. You want to prove them mistaken. But, it is their choice. Their thoughts of you are affecting them a lot more than they are you.

Putting up the effort to shift their position suggests you are enabling them to affect you, your thinking, and your actions. Why give them the satisfaction of getting under your skin?

2. Most people care only about themselves

The trickiest thing for extremely sensitive persons to comprehend is that others frequently don't care about them, or at least not to the extent to which they care about others.

If you are a sensitive person, the trick to not caring is to stop believing that everyone is as considerate as you are. Most people are more worried about themselves than they are about you. They worry about how they seem or how others regard them. Sure, someone may look at you suspiciously, but it is not because they are judging you but because you are terrified, you are condemning them.

3. Care for Yourself

The simplest technique to stop caring so much about what others think is simply worrying about yourself.

Focus on yourself. Care for yourself. Take time to do what you like without worrying about what anyone else may say or think. At first, you may utilize this time alone and in secret to find that you deserve to care for yourself.

Soon you will feel good enough to go out and do it openly.

Go on a bike ride or work out at a gym instead of in your basement. Show the world that you put yourself first. They won't even think about judging you. And if they do, you won't have the time to care.

4. Everybody Does Not Have To Like You

Not everyone has to like you, and not everyone will. It is tough to please everyone. People are so different. To wow them all with your beauty and personality, you will need to stretch so much that you become several persons.

It doesn't matter if some people don't like you. You don't like everyone, do you?

5. The World Does Not Stop Spinning

The world marches on no matter what you do. That is not a bad thing. It is a good thing. If you don't get something done, or if you let someone down, you will wake up tomorrow, and it'll be okay.

Try to put things into perspective. This may help you to stop caring so much. You are not faultless. No one is. You may make blunders and let things slide through the gaps because you are human and whether or not you live up to the standards you set for yourself, you have tomorrow.

6. Consider the Advantages of Not Caring

You bought this book because there is something about caring you don't like. Part of you wants to know how to stop caring. One terrific technique to achieve so is to ponder on the perks that come with not caring.

You will have a degree of independence you can't even think about. You won't be burdened down by others' words or what you interpret their beliefs to be. And you can finally focus on what makes you happy.

7. A Troll Will Always Be Present

There are individuals whose entire objective in life is not to like the most delightful people. There may even be those who will loathe you particularly because they are jealous that everyone else likes you.

Think about it. Even the most well-loved celebrities have internet trolls whose mission in life is to bring them down.

If you base your worth on having everyone like you, it will make you sad and you will always wonder what you are missing.

In fact, when someone doesn't like you, it is their problem, not yours. If you always try your best to be polite and considerate of others, yet if they still don't like you, you know it is not your fault.

8. Always Focus On The Positive

Not everyone is worthy of your efforts. The idea is when someone is not worthy, you try even harder. But, why? There are many folks in the world and in your life who are worthy of your time, energy, and kind nature.

Instead of wasting your time getting the favor of people who don't value your attention, put your effort into the ones that care about you. Don't seek to win them over. Focus on the ones who already know how much you are worth.

9. Filter Out The Bad

You should be ready to break off toxic folks whose negativity immediately rubs off on us when we hang out with them. Whether they are negative or merely bad-mouthing someone, nothing about them enhances your mood or self-esteem.

They are not fulfilling any function in your life, so why are they there?

It might be hard to quit caring, even when someone has done nothing except drag you down. Slowly shut these folks out of your life. Or, if you can manage it, let them know that you believe your relationship has run its course since you are at two separate stages in life.

10. Learn To Say No

Stop believing that saying no makes you a bad person. You are not letting anybody down by putting yourself first. Everyone needs time to decompress and do what they want.

You can't be everything to everyone. It is vital to spend your time and energy on the ideal method and with the relevant individuals.

If someone asks you for a favor that just doesn't feel right, then it is acceptable to say no. If you are fatigued and can't go out to hear your work colleague whine about her partner again, say no.

The reality is that they probably wouldn't feel terrible about saying no to you if the situation were reversed. But that's not even the point. Don't waste your precious time on things you don't enjoy. This is not mean. It is self-care.

11. Help Others in Learning How Not To Care

When you are in the midst of learning how not to care, helping others do the same could feel fantastic. You are getting your good deeds done, but not as a pushover or doormat. You are caring for folks who deserve to learn the same things you've learned.

This enables you to aid those who are in a similar predicament. In the process, you are learning how to take your advice.

12. Condition Yourself

If you find yourself pondering on situations or feeling miserable all the time and sitting and stewing, find an outlet like exercise.

Being able to cope with your pent-up stress and emotions helps assure that you won't explode on the wrong person, make an erroneous assumption, or feel bad about something that's all in your head.

You may even place a hair tie around your wrist and flick yourself if you feel yourself caring too much about what others think.

Finding a constructive and healthy outlet to train yourself away from overthinking and over-caring will assist you to stop worrying about things that aren't significant in the long run.

13. Know That No One is Perfect

Stop believing that you need to be faultless, and accept your weaknesses and blunders as part of life. All the things you've done wrong have made you who you are. You are not faultless, and you don't need to be.

Whether you see someone who makes life seem so easy or appears as if everyone adores them, you simply see a small portion. No one is faultless, no matter how much they may pretend to be, so stop aiming to be. You are you, and that is enough.

14. Refuse to React

When you care when someone is ungrateful or not courteous, you react adversely. When you react to other people, the only one who gets wounded is you. If you want to feel good about yourself, walk away.

Letting someone else's behaviors dictate how you feel about yourself or how you go about the balance of your day gives them authority over you.

You are caring more about what they did than how you are feeling. Put your sentiments ahead of the deeds of others.

15. Stop Trying So Hard

When you care a lot, you try a lot. You try so hard. You seek to impress others. This leads to excessive nervousness. You worry yourself sick. Stop trying so hard, and learning how not to care will follow.

16. Ask Yourself If You Are Happy

Are you happy? Do you feel fulfilled? Do you like yourself? Ask yourself these questions every day. If any answer is no, find out why.

It is likely because you are placing your enjoyment, happiness, and self-image in the hands of others. It is your life, so take control!

17. Surround Yourself with Good Things

I am not one for inspiration or mood boards, but it is the same concept as what I'm saying. Surround yourself with things that make you feel good.

Whether it be a pet, a lovely blanket, or companions who support you, whatever makes you happy should be close.

If you like a fandom like Star Wars or Harry Potter, pick up souvenirs and display them at home. You want to smile at what surrounds you. You don't need to be stylish or hip.

Having items, monetary or otherwise, that make you joyful can naturally help you feel better and shift your care onto healthier, more positive channels.

18. Get Off Social Media

Get off social media immediately. It is no-good for those who care too much. If you want to stop caring, you need to quit allowing yourself to get inundated by posts.

Seeing someone from high school you haven't spoken to in over 10 years talking about something personal might exhaust you. As someone sensitive and caring, you can't help but feel for others, even strangers.

The more you see people, even those you don't know, the more you care. You spend all this emotional energy on people whose lives don't impact you in the least. That may appear selfish. I'm not asking you to ignore everyone or be distant or rude. But if you know that you are prone to care too much, schedule social media time and stay to the limit so you are not overstimulated by it.

19. Stop Judging Others

Before I even start into this, you do criticize individuals. Even if you don't realize it, you do. It can be subconscious. There is a bias you were raised with, whether you believe it or not. Whether it is a touch of racism or sexism, we are all exposed to these things, and they enter into our awareness.

You can't suddenly hit a button and unlearn everything, but taking purposeful efforts to pull back from criticizing individuals even when it is not immediate or visible helps you care less. When you are judging, you are spending effort thinking about others, most commonly in a negative way.

When you do that, your mind quickly believes others are doing the same to you. If you can stop yourself from doing it, your brain won't be prompted to think the same thing.

20. Be Patient

You are not a robot. You cannot stop caring overnight. There is no switch you can turn to learn how not to care. Let yourself come to grips with why you care so much. Take this step by step.

You may even want to contact a therapist to keep yourself on track and work through the underlying reasons why you care so much.

Caring for others is a strength. But, caring too much for others is an invitation to anguish and suffering. With time, dedication, and patience you can learn how to stop caring so much.

People Pleasing

Who is a people pleaser?

A people pleaser is a person who gives a lot of emphasis on pleasing others. And in the process, their major purpose is to be liked and appreciated in return by the people they seek to please.

A people pleaser is never a bad person.

They are neither genuinely manipulative nor are they cheats. But in their enthusiastic pursuit of wanting to please everyone around them, they could go to any degree to acquire someone's affection or admiration, even if it entails arm-twisting someone or silently influencing someone else.

Now everyone has a touch of people-pleasing in them. Almost all of us desire to please someone, meaning to be called a "nice person" or receive a favor back in return from them later. But for most of us, we know where to draw the line.

An overeager people pleaser has no notion that explains where the boundaries of pleasing others stop.

How Do You Become A People-pleaser?

Believe it or not, a lot of the reasons someone might become an excessive people pleaser is how they grew up. Their parents have a lot to do with how much they wish to make other people happy.

On one side, someone's parents may have been abusive in some fashion. As a child, maybe they could never earn the affection of their mother or father – or both. Because of this, they go out of their way to do nice things for others because, unconsciously, they are always attempting to obtain the favor and love of their parents.

This attempt is misdirected, however, as it is not necessarily meant for their parents. And many presumably are not even aware that they are doing this. All they know is that they feel that they have to please others all the time.

Another key reason someone becomes a people pleaser is that they have inadequate self-worth. Since they don't love themselves too much, they are continuously seeking affection from outside - from other people.

So, to feel better about themselves, people pleasers will do just about anything to get other people to admire them. Some are so passionate about it that they entirely forsake their own objectives, wants, and ambitions for other people's. They may not even know who they are anymore as they never care about themselves.

Types of People-Pleasers

There are two categories of human pleasers.

The first people pleaser is the kind who goes out of their way to be nice or help others because they believe that it is their moral purpose to serve others. They can't say no, and they are immensely scared of offending others.

The second type of a people-pleaser is the one where they try to help individuals all the time or consistently acclaim others, to get identical treatment again from their mates.

In all these varieties, the core problem is the same, inadequate self-confidence and low self-esteem.

People pleasers demand others in their existence because they are actually scared of being alone. They demand attention and care and will do anything or say anything to gain it.

Is People Pleasing A Negative Thing?

People-pleasing is not bad. All of us kiss ass now and then to achieve what we want or to be courteous to someone we want to impress.

But there's a tiny line differentiating someone who pleases with a purpose now and then, and someone who does it all the time.

And one glorious day, when your people-pleasing attitude crosses the line, either all your buddies will take you for granted and use you, or they'll see the phony person you are and start ignoring you.

The biggest challenge with people pleasers is the reality that they have no values in life. They morph like a chameleon all the time and become a totally new person depending on who they are spending time with *just to fit in*.

So, if you are a people pleaser, it is something you need to consider. In your continuous effort to satisfy people all the time, you are forsaking your principles in life.

And one beautiful day, you will realize that you don't even know who you are or what you want from your life because you are always changing only to fit in all the time.

Signs That You Are An Overeager People-pleaser

Think through these symptoms with an open mind, and ask yourself if you can relate to them. You may assume you are not an overeager people pleaser, but attempt to seek deep within yourself to realize the genuine person inside you.

After all, there's nothing worse than living in denial.

If you find yourself relating to most of these symptoms of a people pleaser, there's a great probability you are one.

1. You crave praises

You are fairly liberal with your compliments when you are among friends or colleagues with the hope of earning a compliment back from others. Sure, everyone likes getting plaudits, but people-pleasers seek them because they can't commend themselves.

2. You want to be noticed

You feel angry if no one notices your fresh haircut or the new clothing you are wearing to work. Though no one appreciates a dress you are wearing, you feel it looks dreadful on you even though you loved it when you bought it at the store.

3. You lie about your ideals

You don't have your own personality, and you continually say you enjoy something even when you don't like doing it, just to fit in with your group of mates. Your likes and dislikes alter all the time depending on the persons that are around you.

4. You can never say no

You don't like upsetting anyone because you are frightened people may think badly of you if you refuse to help them with anything. And because of this, you overextend yourself by continually saying "yes" to others.

Maybe a friend wants you to aid her to move, but you have a family gathering. You inform her you would help only since you don't know how to say no.

5. You don't care about your loved ones

You give a lot of attention to your new acquaintances or colleagues and try exceedingly hard to satisfy them because you want them to think well of you.

But at the same time, you take the people who love you for granted, as you know they love you unconditionally and will always be there for you regardless of how you act around them or treat them.

6. You are nervous around new companions

You constantly shirk tasks or avoid voicing your views when you are with persons who know you exceptionally well. You work harder with new individuals you are trying to impress, but you become lethargic when it involves only you or someone who already likes you.

You may assume you are being yourself with folks you know well, and don't need to impress them. But you need to recognize that your loved ones will constantly feel that you are taking their devotion for granted as you are always nicer to folks who don't care about you.

7. You always wear a smile

As a people pleaser, you never get angry with your friends or coworkers even if they do something incredibly hurtful. Instead, you push all that wrath inside yourself in the form of implosive anger.

8. Being liked is a priority

You want people to like you wherever you go, and you want everyone you meet to think of you with warm affection.

You consistently strive to display your finest side to everybody you encounter and you always wish that everyone you meet recalls you positively.

9. The judgment of others matter too much

The opinion of other people matters a lot to you and your decision-making. You make your decisions based on other people's wishes.

You encourage all your buddies to express their ideas with you, and you pay more attention to what they say than what you believe is proper.

10. You enjoy attention all the time

You worry about losing friends and you care too much about being liked by everyone. And you can't possibly think of being disliked by others or being lonely.

11. People frequently harm your feelings

You get angry incredibly rapidly when your pals neglect you or leave somewhere without involving you.

Of course, you want to feel loved all the time, but you can't take it when someone considers you are not signed into their lives.

12. The major sacrifices

You sacrifice your enjoyment only to please someone else and earn their favor, or to get a compliment from them. You probably don't even know what makes you happy because you are continuously so obsessed with making other people happy.

13. You can't take criticism

A people pleaser will change their behavior, but they will never realize that they are faulty as it causes them to lose their self-esteem even more. That's why it is challenging to hear criticism when it is aimed your way.

14. You are a liar, even though you would never acknowledge it

You are not honest about who you are, not even to yourself about your likes and dislikes. Your beliefs and ideals fluctuate all the time, just as long as they match those of your new companions that you are seeking to impress.

Even when you feel like something is wrong, you tell yourself that it is fine since your buddies are all doing it.

15. You despise everyone who doesn't like you or perceives you as a fake

A people pleaser does not seek to probe themselves as to why someone else may have this image of you. Instead, you just detest them or speak ill about them because you don't appreciate seeing yourself in a terrible light.

Your self-esteem is bad, hence you don't appreciate it when other people also have unpleasant opinions about you. You get protective.

16. Ps and Qs

You say 'sorry' and 'thank you' without even thinking. You just love saying it because it makes you appear more accommodating and kinder.

Being nice is fine, but not when you are excessively and unnecessarily polite. Polite language gives away your power. For example, if you remark, "Oh I'm sorry, am I bothering you?" Then you give the other person the ability to answer, "Yes you are! Get out of here! "

17. You detest conflict

You spend many restless nights over the simplest quarrel with a new buddy. And you do whatever it takes to make up for it, even if it is not your fault. But you wouldn't do the same for the folks you've already taken for granted.

18. You are too guarded

You don't love losing control of yourself, especially when you are having a drink. Or maybe you have too many secrets, and none of your companions know all your secrets.

You hide the person you are because you don't want people to recognize your inadequacies or your bad side.

19. You offer too much too fast

And many times, others take you for granted. You work too hard to gratify your new companions, and you do everything it takes to ensure that they have a great opinion of you. But quite often, these new companions may conclude up using you and taking advantage of your niceness.

20. You continually fall for flattery

A people pleaser can't resist flattery. And manipulative individuals know how to utilize flattery quite effectively. The flattery could be true, but they fall for any type as it feeds their terrible self-esteem.

When you get in touch with a manipulator, they'll learn to utilize you and squeeze you dry all the time by employing their flattery-request line. "You are really good at doing this. Can you do that for me too? "

21. You don't create limitations

Unfortunately, there are a lot of folks in the world who will take advantage of you if you let them. They will push and push and push those limitations until you scream "no! "

And if you don't ever say no, they keep talking and you keep giving. So, people pleasers don't know how to make boundaries and explain them to other people. "Don't cross this line or you've gone too far" never comes out of their mouths.

Being a people pleaser may feel amazing because it makes you feel appreciated and loved all the time. And as long as you are earning those plaudits, you may not think twice about bending over backward for anyone. But when you are a people pleaser, you are not building any significant relationships. you are only putting on a fake façade that others want to see in you.

Start believing in yourself more. And most importantly, remember that you are an individual and you are who you are. You don't need anyone's approval or praise to make you feel more deserved.

When you totally believe in yourself and accept yourself for the person that you are, you will always lose your people-pleasing desires.

And for the first time in your life, you will start caring more about the individuals who care about you instead of taking them for granted.

Use these signs to find out if you are a people pleaser. And if you recognize that people-pleasing characteristic in you, start believing in your skills and stop depending on the thoughts and comments of others. That makes all the difference.

Setting Personal Boundaries

Learning how to define personal boundaries is crucial for healthy, happy marriages. It is time to focus on what you want versus what you don't want.

When it comes to being happy and healthy in life, learning how to define personal boundaries is crucial. It all comes down to being honest with oneself. If you are going against the things you care about and the things that are crucial to you, tension is never far behind.

In partnerships, limits are critically crucial. If you don't learn to create personal boundaries with others around you, you can discover that individuals overstep the mark frequently. They make you feel uncomfortable, perhaps leading to an unequal relationship.

Of course, you can't expect people to be at blame for this if you don't define and express your bounds. They are not mind-readers, and they don't quickly know what you are content with versus what makes you feel uncomfortable.

Relationships are two-way streets. While setting your limitations, you should listen and respect the personal boundaries of the other person too. This goes for love, business, friend, and family ties!

What Are Personal Boundaries?

Your constraints determine the lines in which you conduct your life. For instance, your boundaries may include spending time alone occasionally. You might be someone who needs alone time to revitalize. Then, make one of your limits your need for the distance a couple of times a week to focus on your self-care needs.

Personal boundaries may involve a large range of various issues, but they are merely limits that you create for yourself and those individuals around you. They educate other people about what you anticipate in a connection of any sort and how you expect to be treated, as well as what you demand. These personal limitations also tell other persons what will happen if they overstep these markers.

Learning to develop personal limitations could be tricky at first. Nobody wants to live by a set of rules. However, forgetting to set your limitations in place leaves you prone to being taken advantage of, and basically living your life for other people and not yourself.

How To Create Personal Boundaries

#1

Think about what is crucial to you and what you need. When you first discover how to build personal boundaries, the first thing to consider is what you need in life and relationships. What is crucial to you and the things you need to be happy and feel positive?

For instance, a personal boundary within a couple may be that you won't accept adultery of any form. It might sound like a no-brainer but if you don't create these restrictions, there are blurry lines as to what you classify as cheating against what you don't. If total loyalty is crucial to you, that's a personal barrier for you.

#2

Spend some time thinking about the border before deciding upon it. You need to be comfortable with the barrier you are creating for yourself and others. So, before you decide upon anything, spend some time thinking about it carefully. Tune into how it makes you feel. Listen to your instincts on this one. If the barrier makes you feel in charge and eager, it is a terrific option. If it makes you feel a little stiff and unclear about which way to travel, it is not the perfect selection for you. Stop and rethink.

You don't want to build a personal boundary with someone in your life and then change your mind and jump to something else. you are just going to confuse others by doing that. While specific restrictions may move a lifetime, you should stick to your fundamental ideals. As a result, you need to be sure of how they make you feel.

#3

Communicate your limitations. This one is difficult! You should explain your limitations clearly and honestly to everyone around you, but how precisely do you do it? it is not the best idea to sit them down and give them a list of things you will and won't accept. However, consider a chat about the things that are essential to you.

When you do speak about your restrictions, make sure that you are specific. Identify your bounds immediately; otherwise, you leave them up for interpretation. Then, if someone breaks one of your limitations, you are going to find yourself in weird waters while having to figure out what to do about it.

#4

Don't allow yourself to feel bad about whatever restriction you've placed in place. Learning how to make personal limitations also means not feeling horrible about something crucial to you. Never allow someone to make you feel bad or crazy about something if it is crucial to you. That's why it is crucial to make sure you think about your limitations before deciding upon them. If they seem right to you, then you shouldn't be compelled to feel bad for having them.

Anyone who makes you feel guilty about a personal boundary you have created is someone who is probably a little furious that they can't just take you for a ride and get what they want out of you nonetheless.

Someone who cares for you will want to work within your restrictions and make you happy while developing a solid bond together.

#5

Make sure you are actually staying to your limitations. Self-awareness is crucial and makes sure that you are truly accomplishing what you promise. You can't make a personal boundary with someone close to you and then go against it by doing the same thing to them! Be consistent. Understand the significance of communication in all sorts of interactions.

#6

Understand the value of self-care. Every boundary you make is about self-care at the core. Not recognizing the benefits of spending time on your own, looking after yourself, and generally being kind to yourself means that you are not fully appreciating the underlying heart of what a personal boundary is.

Make sure that within every relationship you have *friendship, romantic, or otherwise*, you set aside some time for yourself. You are just as valued as everybody else.

Of course, it doesn't suggest you should be selfish. There is a really substantial contrast between the two. Learning how to build personal boundaries shouldn't suggest that you are being unkind or unreasonable to anyone else, but it does mean that you are sticking to whatever is necessary for you.

#7

Stick to the consequences of your restrictions. Personal limits suggest that not only do you set out the norms of what you expect, but you also talk about what will happen if those personal boundaries are not followed. That doesn't mean you walk away at the first sense of someone making a mistake or overstepping the line. It does take discussing and being clear that going against your limitations is not something you are willing to accept.

It could be hard to be strong in these times. While it is crucial to remember that everyone makes faults, if it is a common occurrence, they are taking advantage and not simply someone making a mistake.

It is only normal to give a fuck what other people think of you. It is only natural to crave the approval of other people. But there are huge implications connected with doing so.

When you give too much fucks about what others think of you, you end up feeling uneasy in public spaces.

When you seek validation through dating (and receiving attention from women), you wind yourself on an emotional roller coaster that could leave you feeling 'unworthy' and lonely.

When you give too many fucks what your family thinks about your career, you end up working at a job you don't care about.

Quit Seeking approval

#1: Understand Why it Doesn't Matter

The first step is to realize why it is fruitless to worry about the perceptions of other people. You need to realize precisely how self-conscious the common human is. Seriously, even the most confident males worry about how other people regard them.

It is why we spend so much time selecting what we're going to wear. It is why we go to the gym. It is why we get cool-ass hairstyles. And that is why we desire to make a lot of money and become famous.

The entire concept of fame, and what makes it so attractive, is that it promises that lots of other people will adore you.

So next time you find yourself fearing that everyone is gazing at you and judging you, consider that they are probably too busy worrying about what other people are thinking about them to even notice you.

The 'High' of Approval Does Not Last
Here's another essential thing you need to understand: the 'high' you feel after receiving permission NEVER lasts.

Get that massive promotion? Congrats, you will feel quite important for a few days. Then you will be back at it, chasing the approval of your boss again.

She finally texted you back? Congrats, you will feel good about yourself for a few hours. Then you will be back at it, anxiously anticipating the next response.

Receive a fantastic compliment? Congrats, you will walk with swagger for a few minutes. Then you will be back at it, anxious about what everyone thinks of you.

I don't aim to be a 'Debbie Downer' here, winning acceptance does feel wonderful. But it is like a drug.

If you depend on obtaining approval to feel good about yourself, then you will continuously be pursuing it. you will never feel happy or 'complete' without it.

And you will always give far too much fucks what other people think of you.

If you are having a wonderful day and people are paying you attention, then everything is fine. But if you are alone for the day or someone looks at you incorrectly, then you feel like a useless piece of garbage. This gets me to point #2.

#2: Build a Lifestyle You Can Be Proud of

The best way to stop giving a fuck is to start living a life that YOU can be proud of... regardless of what other people think. And this all starts with good daily practices.

Develop the Right Habits for YOU

I'm not talking about washing your teeth, making your bed, and flossing. No, I'm talking about routines that allow you to live up to your standards.

For me, this means doing activities like lifting weights, practicing martial arts, playing basketball, writing, meditating, and traveling often. I do these things because I enjoy doing them. I do things because I feel delighted when I do them.

This way, it doesn't matter if someone rejects me. Or if any dude disrespects me. Or if I receive a lot of unpleasant comments on one of my blogs or YouTube videos...

No, I don't give a FUCK about any of these things!

And it is all because I know that I can still hit the gym. Or go on a little trip to meet my pals in Colombia. Or get engaged in intense meditation. Or join in a summer league basketball game.

No matter what other people think of me, I can always take solace in knowing that I've established a lifestyle that I'm proud of.
And it is something that no one can take from you.

Set Goals YOU Care About
While adopting the perfect habits is the #1 thing you can do to 'self-validate' and quit

giving a fuck what other people think, it is equally vital to have the RIGHT aims.

It is so easy to slip into the trap of establishing goals that fit other people, and what you assume THEY want you to do...

But when you do this, you slice off your balls and give them over to someone else. Seriously, you repress your wants and substitute them for someone else's. You give other people the authority to decide YOUR life's direction.

So how can you avoid this mistake?

Easy, you avoid establishing super-long-term targets and instead focus on building moderate-term goals (think 1-6 months) that match your current interests and desires.

You see, other people tend to urge you (directly and on a subconscious level) to live up to their long-term aspirations for you. By focusing on shorter-term goals, you effectively let yourself concentrate totally on YOUR aspirations, while gently 'pushing aside' the interests and ideas of other people.

#3: Catch Yourself Seeking Approval

Catch Yourself in the Moment
Even when you structure your life around habits and goals that you actually care about, you are still prone to give a toss about what other people think.

The idea is to catch oneself giving in to the act of too many fucks. It doesn't matter if you are at work, and you discover yourself worried about whether or not your boss is displeased with you. Or if you want to ask a woman out, and you find yourself over-analyzing whether or not she likes you. Or if you are at a party, and you notice yourself worrying about whether or not the other party-goers think you are a cool man.

Regardless of the circumstance, do these 3 acts to break the pattern and stop giving a fuck.

Catch yourself. The most critical thing is to confess that you are giving a fuck about what others think, or seeking their favor.

Accept it. The natural thing is to lie to yourself and tell yourself that you are not actually seeking acceptance. Don't do this. Instead, embrace it and convince yourself that everything's going to be okay.

Let it go. It doesn't matter exactly WHY you are giving a fuck. The main thing is to let it go. And the simplest technique to do this is to focus on breathing 4-5 deep 'belly' breaths.

This will be tough at first, but the more you find yourself giving a fuck, the simpler it will be to let it go. And then you may go back to enjoying your life... with ZERO fucks given!

The wonderful thing about this method is that it will become a natural, subconscious process over time (i.e. you will gently teach your brain to stop giving a fuck) (i.e. you will slowly retrain your brain to stop giving a fuck) (i.e. you will slowly retrain your brain to stop giving a fuck).

Take a minute RIGHT NOW to question yourself why you are doing certain things like living in that certain place or why you have the interests that you have.

If your response is because your spouse wants you to do it, or because you feel it will impress your friends, then pay heed! Structuring your life around the expectations and preferences of others is a formula for catastrophe.

It will erode your self-esteem and compel you to continually seek approval from other people. It will make you give way too many fucks.

Understand that it is futile to worry about what other people think as the 'high' of getting their approval never lasts anyway. Build a lifestyle that YOU can be proud of by practicing activities that make YOU happy and establishing targets that YOU care about.

Build the habit of finding yourself seeking praise, receiving it, and then letting it go, and enjoy the FREEDOM that comes with not giving a fuck (and turning only to yourself for approval)!

How To Give Zero Fucks

Knowing how to not give a fuck genuinely needs a little practice. It could be challenging not to care, to shrug things off, and to let things go.

But if you have acquired the talent of not giving a fuck, it may genuinely feel very liberated, and make you a better person as a result.

So how can you learn how to not give a fuck? Let's take a look at some of the things you need to complete.

1. Understand what it entails

Not giving a fuck is not actually about not caring about anything at all. That's a widespread misperception that people often get wrong.

There is a difference between not caring, and choosing you don't give a fuck, which then motivates you to take something.

It may be 'hell yeah I'm going to audition for this play because I don't give a fuck about if my friends might laugh at me or my mother doesn't believe I can do it.' Or, 'I will apply for that job that sounds much too advanced for me because I don't give a fuck, and is it going to be that horrible if I don't get it?

Not giving a fuck is kind of like permanently having the mentality of 'I've got nothing to lose.'

If you can focus on that and understand that if you just loosened up, said goodbye to your fears, and seized life by the balls, some genuinely amazing things may happen to you - so just go for it!

2. Learn what is necessary and what is not

To be able to know how to not give a fuck, you are genuinely going to have to uncover what is significant to you and what is not.

It is silly to purposefully strive and not care about anything. But at the same time, it is vital to determine what things matter to you. Focus on them continually and just forget the rest.

If you are always focused on your aims and striving for your goals, you won't give a fuck about anything else. You won't allow anyone to come in your way, and you will scream 'to hell with the consequences! '

You won't give a fuck about the things that are not crucial to you. So, the next time that you don't obtain what you desire or something you believed you would, actually step back and weigh it up.

Does it matter? Do you genuinely care? If the answer is 'not really' then just decide to not give a fuck and get on with your life - it is as simple as that!

3. Get to know yourself

Getting to know oneself well is highly crucial when it comes to not giving a fuck. If you don't know what is essential to you, then you can end up making errors.

Having a terrible attitude, being slow, or purposefully refusing to do or care or realize anything because you are attempting to injure someone or seek revenge on them simply is not the path forward.

Besides, then everyone will see right through you too, and there is nothing worse than pretending you don't give a fuck when you genuinely do.

If you are not convincing, then you will simply finish up seeming like an idiot. That's why it is so crucial to get to know yourself, get in touch with your thoughts and feelings, and fully accept that it is natural to feel and to care – so don't strive to deny yourself that.

4. Weigh up the implications

One other immensely vital thing to remember when it comes to knowing how not to give a fuck, is that you need to think about the ramifications of your actions all the time.

It is all well and good not giving a fuck about things, but if you damage everyone and everything in your path - is it worth it?

You cannot give a fuck about most things without damaging other people, so always try to remember that – and also be really sure you are not going to have any regrets, or this is not going to come back and strike you in the ass another time.

5. Grow A Thicker Skin

Not giving a fuck is also about having thick skin. You don't have to become a heartless robot or anything. But at the end of the day, if you are the sort of person who wears their heart on their sleeve and continually gets quite emotionally sensitive about things, it is going to be challenging to adopt an attitude of not caring about things.

Try to accept the thought that disappointing, unpleasant things happen to everyone, so you need to build a thicker skin if you want to be better at not caring about them.

6. Be comfortable with it

If you don't give a fuck, you have to own it. At first, it could feel a little odd, it might look disrespectful or bad somehow.

But the more you practice the art of not giving a fuck the more you will begin to feel comfortable with it, and the more you will realize that it is not just about being rude or acting like you couldn't care less about anything.

It is about concentrating on what is most important to you, stopping at nothing when it comes to accomplishing your aims, and not letting negativity or failures stand in the way of you enjoying your life.

7. Be confident in your choices

If you decide you don't give a fuck, you have to really believe in yourself. Once you have made that decision, there is no turning back. So, be confident and true to yourself.

To gain that air of 'no fucks given,' you have to come across as confident and all in - then you will have discovered what not giving a fuck is all about and can lead a better, healthier, more productive life.

8. Stop looking for approval

The next time you are selecting your life, don't run it past anyone.

Try this once and trust yourself to make the best choices for your life. We typically depend on family or friends to persuade us we are on the straight track, but it may be destructive in the long run.

By asking for permission or approval from other people, we are telling ourselves that we don't know how to continue and that diminishes our efforts.

If you want to quit caring about what other people think and start living your own life, stop seeking others to bring insight into your life.

Self-esteem won't be boosted unless you wise up and take responsibility. Responsibility permits you to take action to improve yourself and help others. And self-esteem goes both ways. If you are relying on external validation like praise from other people to fuel your self-esteem, then you are giving over authority to others.

Instead, start establishing stability within. Value yourself and who you are.

9. Do tasks that make you happy

If you want to avoid caring about what other people think and start living your own life in a way that lights you up, stop doing things you don't want to do.

We all feel the pressure of having to say yes to an invitation, but if you don't want to attend dinner or a party, don't go.

Do activities that make you delighted. The more you do for yourself, the better you will feel.

And no, it is not selfish to reject a party invitation if that is not truly how you want to spend your time.

If more individuals imposed restrictions on how they employed their time, people would be a lot happier.

A lot of these challenges come from the fact that we feel pleasure is caused by outside relationships.

This is something that is not easy to realize.

For example, many of us may believe that pleasure implies getting a dazzling new iPhone or receiving a greater promotion at work for more money. It is what society tells us every day! Advertising is everywhere. But we need to know that happiness alone exists inside ourselves.

Outside attachments give us temporary satisfaction - but after the experience of excitement and joy is over, we go back to the cycle of chasing that high again.

An extreme example exhibiting the consequences of this is a drug addict. They are joyful while they are taking drugs, but sad and enraged when they are not. It is a loop that no one wants to become lost in.
True happiness can only come from within.

It is time to take control back and acknowledge that we produce pleasure and inner calm inside ourselves.

10. Pay attention to why you do or say things

Whenever you make a choice, realize that there are a set of beliefs behind that decision that may be holding you back or driving you forward.

If you are making decisions that keep you small, ask yourself who you may be thinking about when you make that decision.

We all have folks in our lives we desire to impress upon or whom we want approval from, but it is vital not to let their influence over us affect our choices in life.

Parents are a wonderful instance of how much indirect effect they may have, even after we've become grownups.

Are you in a job you detest because your mother thinks you are a good accountant?

Time to break free from that clutch and decide what you want to do for yourself.

We only get life once, thus we must endeavor to have the greatest good effect that we can, however that may like for you.

11. Look for anything worth giving a fuck

Okay, here's the thing:

People cannot learn how to not give a fuck if they don't have a clear objective in life.

In other words, you have to dedicate your fucks to something to stop caring about everything.

Because let's face it: You won't have any fucks to give if you were focused on one essential objective.

You won't care about the regular political fighting.
You won't give a fuck about what your colleagues are speaking about.

So think about what you want to achieve:

— Do you want to learn Spanish?
— Do you want to start a new business?

There are many more things you may imagine for yourself - what is important is something dear to you.

The key to a happy, satisfying life is learning where and when to give a fuck. You are not going to live forever.

You need to be intelligent about your brief time in the world. So enjoy life while you can.

Don't allow your intellect to get clouded by tiny problems that are not significant in the larger scheme of things.

Stop worrying about what other people think and start focusing on what you think. It is not simple, and you will fall up plenty of

times as you strive to get your act together,
but it is worth the effort.

How To Quit Worrying About Unimportant Things

#1 Remember that there are very few things that vital in life

You fundamentally know what these things are, and they are pretty clear.

A good way to figure out what those things are is to fast forward time and see yourself on your deathbed and what would be going through your thoughts.

On the question of what dying people regret, research suggests that it is largely connected to the time they did not spend with their loved ones and instead spent on pointless occupations, attempting to live up to other people's expectations, and going after things they believed would bring them pleasure.

#2 Understand that you have a limited number of fucks to provide

While we can all recognize the truth in point #1 above, it is challenging to maintain it at the forefront throughout our busy, demanding lives (and also unhealthy to be perpetually imagining yourself on your deathbed, but that's beside the point).

Examining Maslow's Hierarchy of Needs demonstrates that things like guaranteeing a roof over our heads and placing food on our tables, feeling safe and secure, and having a family pretty about cover the force of satisfaction in our lives.

Yet we are exhausted and frustrated because we detour from focusing our attention on what is actually important.

Instead, we squander our fucks by freaking out on useless things like gossip, fighting in traffic jams, fixating on the past, cleaning our crowded homes that are loaded with superfluous items, or agonizing over a mistake or an offhand word we can't take back

#3 Realize that other people are always teaching you what to worry about

In addition to all of the time-sucking things we intentionally sign ourselves up to care about, we have a whole set of additional time-sucking activities that other people strive to put onto us.

It is very hard to say no to a mentor who wants you to spend more time networking and "building your brand" when you are craving meaningful contacts at work. It is challenging to say no to a colleague who needs your time, energy, and support for a new firm when all you want is to carve out time to attend a yoga class.
It is annoying to say no to contributing your money to a skincare pyramid scheme your

pal joined when you are pleased with your existing face wash, thank you very much.

It is as challenging to say "no" to suggestions, advice, and opinions about what you should be doing, how you should be spending your time, or what you should actually value.

#4 Know that listening to them occupies your time, attention, and pleasure

Instead of saying no to these non-value-added tasks and undesired offers, you feel awful and do all of the above and consider the ideas that don't line up with your ideals.

You have zero energy left to give a fuck about the things that matter after you have wasted your precious time worrying about all the idiotic things you cannot control.

If you are like me, you tend to stress about these things even if you do recognize that they don't important. I spend a large amount of time wondering, which is another thing that detracts from appreciating the present and the things in my life that are worth my efforts. Time is our solitary limited resource and it is our obligation to utilize it wisely.

#5 Get comfortable saying no and turning people off if you actually want to change

Spending your time and attention on things that don't provide value to your life throws everything off balance, causes extra stress and agony, and eventually stops you from having the most fulfilling experiences possible. You have to make a purposeful decision to change, learn to start saying no, and stop giving a fuck on the things that aren't genuinely essential.

Implementing this in real life is tough to do as not everyone is going to love your sudden lackadaisical attitude toward what they want you to care about.

Mastering The Art Of Giving Zero Fucks

1. Quit Facebook and any other sorts of social media that makes you care about silly things

Seriously, it is non-value-added and you will be astonished how people are still able to contact you by utilizing other forms of communication. No one will artificially remember your birthday, but the nicest gift will be forgetting the names of folks whom you should have deleted from memory in 8th grade. I've been off the 'book since 2012 and can honestly say that when individuals complain about seeing ultrasound images of the fetuses of faraway pals, I cannot understand.

2. Offload all of the duties you presently have but don't want.

Also, opt out of any extra activities that you feel obligated to partake in but don't completely appreciate the advantages. We're told never to give up in any situation, and I feel this is garbage. So does Mark Manson. Giving up the correct things may make you free! Or, at least will set your time free to reinvest in something you actually care about.

3. Train yourself to say no in new ways

When someone provides a suggestion or presents advice that you don't appreciate, merely answer "Thank you for your insight, I'll consider it" and don't allow it to take root in your mind. If someone asks you to do something that you don't want to do: say, "Thank you for thinking of me for this. Let me examine it and come back to you." Then, simply follow up with a simple, polite ", no, thank you."

While these tips aid with the evident things that you don't want, and that you know drain your time and energy, it is crucially necessary to clarify what you do desire.
People who are not clear on what they want out of life, or what they actually value, will

not be able to master the delicate art of not giving a fuck. You have to be clear on what you want to filter out all the other garbage.

Once you understand that you don't need to worry about what other people say, you will be free to live life the way you desired from the start.

You see, understanding how to not give a fuck is all about devotion. It is about not paying attention to things that aren't important.

So strive for your enormous dreams!
Stop giving fucks!
Your time is vital - spend it on things that are worth your while!

Author's Note

I hope you've learned one or two things reading this book. If you have, make sure to leave a rating and/or review on the Amazon store. It goes a long way for indie authors like me. Thank you for purchasing this book.

www.ingramcontent.com/pod-product-compliance
Lightning Source LLC
Chambersburg PA
CBHW051436150726
48000CB00005B/2122